So I asked, "Lord, Why Me?" He answered, "Why Not You?"

My Journey with the Lord

Autumn Cannon, M.Ed

Why Not Me
By Autumn Cannon

No part of this book may be reproduced or transmitted in any form without written permission from the author except for the inclusion of brief quotations in review.

Copyright © 2015

Published in the United States of America

Cover design and Photography by *Blusuede Photography*

Edited By *Critique Editing Services*

ISBN 978-0-9961536-5-2

Disclaimer

In this book, I will share with you my personal conversations with God and important things He has shared with me about my life in my quiet time and in my dreams.

My goal is to give you hope to hold on to your dreams and goals in life. I want to inspire you to go deeper in your relationship with Christ and let him guide you. Communing with Him is very rewarding.

The information in this book is provided strictly for inspirational and motivational purposes. Some locations and names have been changed to protect the identity of the participants.

Dedication

I dedicate this book in remembrance of my paternal grandparents, R. S. and Ina Cannon, who passed away in 2009 and 2014, respectively. They taught me to always follow my dreams, listen to God, and keep myself educated. They said education is a continual process. They are the reason I am who I am today. My grandfather wrote the first book in my immediate family, then challenged me to do the same. I wish they could be here to share in this milestone. They were my biggest cheerleaders and always pushed me. Every chance they got, they bragged on their family.

This book is also, in remembrance of my grandfather, Alfred Fisher, who passed away from cancer in 1990. I see his face and mile spirit in his children, my uncle, aunts, and my mom.

To my beautiful maternal grandmother, Clotea Fisher, the one who is older in age but looks younger than her own daughters, I love you! I will always remember the practical advice and steps for living life you taught me. You taught me to be wise and not stupid! You have such a sweet spirit and a servant's heart. You also encouraged me to be unselfish.

To my parents, Harold and Gwendolyn Cannon, who taught me how to spend time with Christ by your example. I saw my parents reading their Bibles daily. Thanks for our family Bible studies. I am who I am because of God through you!

Acknowledgements

First, giving honor to my Lord and Savior, Jesus Christ. I am honored to have such a wonderful Savior. Daily, I stand in awe of You!

To my crazy brothers, Kenny, Seth, and Micah who always keep laughter in our family. You jokesters have always kept my spirits up without even knowing half of what I was going through. You were just being yourselves.

To my one and only sister, Amy Cannon Bryant and brother-in-law, Enoch Bryant. I love you for taking me in during my valley experiences.

To my sisters-in-law, Penny Cannon and Rosalia Cannon, thank you for your awesome spirits of sisterly love, you have poured upon me.

Table of Contents

Introduction

Chapter 1...He Chose Me

Chapter 2...Save My Son

Chapter 3...Changing Lanes

Chapter 4...New Direction

Chapter 5...Houston Journey

Chapter 6...Birthing Destiny

Chapter 7...Unfaithful

Chapter 8...Back for Validation

Chapter 9...Unprepared for the Game

Chapter 10...Transportation Thief

Chapter 11...My Wedding

Chapter 12...Tool Store Vacation

Chapter 13...Enemy at the Court

Chapter 14...My Best Friend

Chapter 15...My Husband or Not

Chapter 16 ....The Pool Experience

Chapter 17...Showtime

Conclusion

Poem

Foreword

Not often can you find a riveting, life changing, read all in one book. Ladies and Gentleman we have found the author who can vividly share her life story in such a way that will encourage you, and laugh your socks off in the same breath.
Autumn Cannon's life has been enriched with an anointing that will touch you at your very core. She delightfully allows the reader to enter in her zany mind, while keeping you enthralled as every page turns.
I've been pleasured to sing with her, traveling in and out of the country. Whether singing, writing, playwriting, directing, or composing she is a PHENOMENAL woman that has triumphed many road blocks and obstacles, but somehow, she has kept her sense of wit. Sit back, kick your shoes off(if they don't stink too bad) and enjoy the read of a lifetime!

HATS OFF TO "WHY NOT ME"
-Dana Lemear

Introduction

I accepted Christ into my life at a very young age. I was nine years old and understood exactly what I was doing when my parents led me in the prayer of life! I remember being so excited because my mom always spoke about this amazing God who did great things and could help us through all of our problems! I watched my parents' relationship with each other and their relationship with God as they focused on Him, which caused them to focus on each other. Their Bibles never closed. I mean literally, my dad's Bible would stay open near his chair until he returned to it the next day for more reading. My mom's Bible had lots of notes and was really worn from use. My mom would pray about things and then share with us her testimony about what God did for her and for our family.

I remember having ankle pain one day; my mom laid her hands on my ankle and asked the Lord to remove the pain and within two minutes, it was gone! I thought, *I really want to get to know the One behind these miracles.* I kept wondering, *How is my mom so tight with the Lord? He must really favor her.* One day I asked my mom, "How can I tap into this favor?" She made it plain and simple, "Choose Christ."

I began to have my own relationship with the Father. I would read and read the Bible but for some reason, it was very hard to understand. I asked myself, *How am I supposed to get to know God, if I don't understand His language?* My mom told me to pray before I read and ask God for wisdom, knowledge, and understanding of His Word. She was right. It worked! I began to understand God's Word like never before. It was like the words on the pages were literally jumping out at me and causing feelings and lots of brain activity! I began to hear His still, small voice in my life. I became addicted to communicating with God.

Eventually, I was led to read about all of the people in the Bible who were dreamers, to learn how and why God communicated with them. I had always been a dreamer, and I began to focus on my dreams to see if God wanted to communicate with me through them as well. Sometimes people are skeptical and they don't believe that dreams are one of the ways that God can speak to us. I say to those people, there are many examples of this in God's Word.

I am honored to bring to you, my intimate conversations with our heavenly Father so that you too can understand and trust Him. Most of my life, I have wondered why He uses me for His work. The answer is simple, Why not you, Autumn? God really does speak to us and give us instructions, if only we would listen. He speaks to me in dreams and confirms it in His Word. I will share it with you.

Daniel 1:17
"As for these four youths, God gave them learning and skill in all literature and wisdom, and Daniel had understanding in all visions and dreams." (NIV)

Also
Job 33:14-16, Matthew 2:12, and Matthew 27:19.

Chapter 1
He Chose Me

I am so honored that God chose me. He chose to love me unconditionally. My God and I have a special relationship. I love the time that we spend together. All of the intimate moments are great whether it is 3:00 a.m., when He wakes me up to talk or 3:00 p.m. in the middle of the day. Just like any earthly relationship whether friendship, marriage, or a dating relationship, spending time with each other helps you to grow closer. We began to recognize each other's voice in a crowd. We also knew how the other would feel or react in certain situations. So I learned at an early age to try to consistently spend time with my Lord. I was nine years old when I accepted Christ as my personal Savior. There is a misconception that God does not deal with us in small day-to-day issues, but I believe He is passionate in His desire to help us in all areas of our lives and wherever we need Him. God really helps with day-to-day operations, as well as life's big experiences. I am glad that God chooses to speak to me in dreams. He speaks to people in many different ways. Our Father speaks to us through our hearts and minds. God occasionally speaks audibly to His children, but He will always confirm what He says in His word. We must not forget to take it upon ourselves to pick up the Bible and search for confirmation.

I can remember as far back as when I was a little girl, big dreams were always a part of my sleep experience. I would wake up with happy feelings, remembering the movie that played out in my head the previous night. Sometimes, I would become fascinated with going to sleep and dreaming. I truly believe that God chose this avenue of speaking to me and giving me warnings in my life. It wasn't until I experienced the biggest storm in my life that I began to pay close attention to my dreams. I felt like God was nudging me saying, "Hear My voice." As I got older, I began to also have visions while awake, which most of us call daydreaming. This is another avenue God uses to speak to me. When I think about the various avenues of communication, I can't help but think about how omnipotent God is to be able to show up in my thoughts! I don't even have to speak it and He is in my head.

Now don't get me wrong, I know that sometimes our dreams can come from things that we experience or want to experience, and then our brain spits out the visions. I believe that the enemy can also send us dreams. I make a conscious effort to pay attention and listen for the Lord's voice. My relationship with God helps me to know the difference and gives me focus.

Life has been good at times and difficult at other times. During those difficult times we all need some type of guidance. We have been given free choice for our decisions in life. I often wonder why God allowed me to have such a great upbringing, but then let me go through so many storms in my adult life. I am not perfect, so I don't expect to have only good in my life, but I also wonder, *God, why are you so good to me in guiding me through these storms?* He simply answered, "Autumn, why not you?" I knew then it is because He trusts me to help others with my testimonies, and lead them to Him.

Isaiah 30:21

"Whether you turn to the right or to the left, your ears will hear a voice behind you, saying, "This is the way; walk in it." (NIV)

Chapter 2

Save My Son

Dream:

I was sweeping my kitchen floor one day in my cute little house in Jackson, Mississippi. Out of the corner of my eye, I noticed a little black boy about the age of seven staring at me with the saddest little face. His lips were moving but I couldn't hear what he was saying. As I walked closer to him to see what was wrong, I could hear him saying, "I am dead and I don't know why. Please tell me why I am dead, please help me." I felt so sorry for the little boy. My heart ached, I wanted to help him so badly. He wanted to know who killed him. Forget the fact that this little boy just showed up in my home out of the blue. I just wanted to help him. All of a sudden, my mind went into rewind mode as if the little boy and I were traveling back in time. We traveled really fast just like when you're watching a movie and someone has pressed the rewind button.

I was sitting in my living room waiting for my live-in boyfriend to come home from work. He was a police officer and was always in uniform. He was tall, dark, and slightly handsome. It was obvious that he was physically and verbally abusive towards me, but I always thought that it was because of something I did. That was the reason I stayed. I mean, I am not perfect, but I didn't deserve for him to be so mean and unloving towards me. He was really good at apologizing, though. The biggest problem in our relationship was the fact that he did not like my seven-year-old son. *This happens in many blended families*, I thought, *they will eventually get along. We will just hang in there and make it work.*

One day, we began to argue and fight physically. This was the day that the light bulb went on in my head and I felt that I'd had enough. My thinking was, *Now I am strong enough to leave.* I didn't care what would happen to me but, I needed to save my son's life. I grabbed my son by the hand, and we ran out of the side door to my little, light blue, raggedy car. My son climbed into the back seat. As I got into the driver seat, I realized I did not have my car keys. I thought, *I must get back inside to get the keys,* but when I looked up at the door of the house, my boyfriend was standing there. I yelled to my son to get out of the car and run. I grabbed his hand and we took off running down the street. My boyfriend began chasing us with a gun. All I could think of was protecting my son from this evil man. We ran as fast as we could, yelling for help with no destination in mind. No one came to our rescue. People were passing by probably thinking this was all a game.

Out of nowhere, I felt a strong urge to fight back. I grabbed my son's hand tighter, we stopped running, turned around and charged back towards my boyfriend. I felt super human strength as I grabbed the gun from his hand and began to fight back. My son and I then ran back towards our house. The only thing on my mind was to protect him from the enemy. We ran back inside the house to look for the car keys. I at least wanted to get my son safely out of that neighborhood. My boyfriend made it to the front door as we headed out of the back door and made it to the car. I cranked it and began to back out of the driveway. He stood behind the car to try and stop me. That was the wrong thing to do because I that moment, my state of mind was to run over him. I had to stop him from coming after us. It was a scary situation. The evil in his eyes was bone chillingly scary.

It was early in the morning so I took my son to school. I figured it was the safest place for him at the moment. Also, I needed to be alone so that I could get back to the house and settle things. When I arrived back home, the house was empty. His things were gone and so was his car. I was excited to see that I could possibly have a new start. I began to clean up the mess we made from our earlier fight. One hour later, I received a call from the school saying that my son had left school. He was picked up by my boyfriend. The secretary from the school said my son willingly chose to go with him as he signed him out at the school's office.

Later I discovered that my boyfriend had kidnapped and murdered my boy. I couldn't believe it. I couldn't protect him from the enemy. Why would my son choose to go with him? I did all I could to protect him.

Real Life:

This dream was a warning for what was about to happen in my life. A warning of what I was about to lose. It was seven o'clock in the morning, I looked over at my husband of two years, still asleep. He looked so innocent and loving. I wanted to push out of my mind all of the turmoil that we were going through in our marriage. I just wanted to stare at him forever in his innocent state. He awakened, said good morning while staring. He said, "I am tired of trying to be a good man. Good is not in me. I want to release you so you can find someone who makes you happy." He decided that he didn't want to be married anymore. I thought it was a temper tantrum because of our current situation, which was figuring out what my step-daughter was going to wear for her pictures at school that morning. I didn't think much of it when he made the comment. I proceeded to fix breakfast and left the house.

I drove to work as usual. It was a normal day at the radio station. The jazz music was pleasurable as it always was. My co-workers were all in a good mood. We laughed throughout the day. I was visited by my good friend, Faye who revealed to me that she had just gotten her own apartment. "I am so excited for you, Faye," I said. We rejoiced for a while and I let her know that I was proud of her and how far she had come. She said she was confused because she felt the Holy Spirit told her to get a two bedroom apartment. I asked, "Were you obedient?" She said, "Of course." Little did I know that this was the beginning of a wonderful journey into my addiction to Christ.

Later that evening I arrived home from work to fix dinner for my husband and stepchild. When I pulled up, there was a huge U-Haul truck on the lawn. I was so confused and wondered who was leaving. I walked up to the door only to find that my husband was packing the U-Haul. I didn't know he was serious about not wanting to be married anymore. I felt my chest tighten; I couldn't breathe, and I was getting dizzy. Could this really be happening to me? Is my husband leaving me? Am I becoming a statistic?

Did I do something wrong? Am I not good enough? Is it another woman? I questioned myself over and over and over.

I called my friend, Faye to tell her what was happening. She immediately called the rest of our friends. Faye said, "Autumn, I know why the Holy Spirit told me to get the extra room; it is for you." Faye invited me to stay and all of my friends told me not to bring anything. I was instructed to only bring the important stuff and leave everything else behind. They said, "You are going to start a new life and we will help you." Tears began to roll down my face as I thought to myself, *I really have some great friends!* I sat on my bed at midnight trying to figure out what just happened. *Ten hours ago, I had a husband, a home, and a step-child. Now I have nothing and I am staring at the walls, alone wondering why God allowed this to happen to me*, I said to myself. I reached out to any and everyone who I thought could help me. I was embraced by several women of God who prayed for me and spoke positive things into my life. These women prayed for me and interceded on my behalf because at this time, I could not hear anything from God. I was numb to feelings of any kind. I would awaken at 2:00 a.m. with crying and screaming in my heart and then a text message would come from one of my friends. She knew I was up and she knew what was wrong. Yes, she had interceded in prayer on my behalf. God would awaken her every time I was at my worst. Her messages were right on time and really ministered to me in my time of need. She shared that somehow she could feel my pain. She literally felt the heart pounding horror and loneliness that I felt each day, which resulted in her praying harder for me. Another lady from the church who had been through the same experience was praying for me as well. She told me to ask God what I was supposed to take or learn from this situation. The night I asked, I fell asleep and began to dream.

Interpretation:

I was suffering in my marriage during the time of this dream. My ex-husband was very mean and unfaithful. I knew the enemy was after him because that is what Satan does. He tries to attack the head of the household. I always felt like a mother figure to my ex-husband anyway, because I was more spiritually mature and had experienced more positive things in life than he had, so he looked to me to teach him. I tried to pray for him and shield him from the enemy every day. He had a little boy's mentality. My ex had always acted like a little boy in the Spirit. In the dream, the boyfriend represented the enemy chasing us. The enemy felt that by taking my heart or what I loved most, he could get me as well.

Three months later, I literally saw the enemy take my

ex-husband's mind and destroy our marriage. He divorced me, saying he was tired of trying to be a good man. He wanted to be bad. He chose to do what the enemy wanted him to do. I thought, *we were doing so well, for the past 4 months, he wasn't cheating and we were getting along very well. Why all of a sudden, is it over?* I think it is so amazing how God thought enough of me to communicate with me and clarify the storm. He wants to spend time with us in conversation daily. There are so many things that God wants to tell us. We just get so wrapped up in our own worlds that we do not make time to hear his voice. God gave us the power and strength to fight back when we get into sticky situations! We sometimes simply choose not to listen. We have free choice but the enemy cannot overtake us unless we allow him to. I decided at that moment that throughout this process, I was determined not to let the enemy have any power in this situation. It is Jesus Christ all the way!

Luke 10:19

"Behold, I give you the authority to trample on serpents and scorpions, and over all the power of the enemy, and nothing shall by any means hurt you." (NKJV)

Chapter 3

Changing Lanes

I was driving down a busy three-lane highway one spring evening after leaving work. I was taking my usual route home, which was to take a right turn ahead at the traffic light. I had it planned out in my mind as usual, turning from the right lane was going to be my next move. Just before my turn, there was a bus stopped in the right lane, delivering passengers. I thought to myself, in order for me to make this right turn, I should turn in front of the bus before it begins to move. I heard a still, small voice saying, "Move all the way over to the far left lane." I said to the Holy Spirit, "That doesn't make sense, especially since I am getting ready to make a right turn once I pass this bus." He said, "Change lanes now, all the way to the far left." I argued with the Holy Spirit for a second, as we all do.

I eventually switched lanes and ended up in the far left lane, fearing that I would miss my turn ahead, because I was wasting time in the left lane. As soon as I switched, I looked to my right and just ahead of me a young boy, approximately 14 years old came running from in front of the bus. Without stopping or looking both ways, he sprinted from the right lane to the middle lane and was headed to the left lane. He was running fast and

I was driving about 56 mph. I quickly realized that there was no time for me to stop before hitting him. I stomped my brakes really hard and screamed as my car slid and hit the boy. He hit the windshield, rolled over the top of my car and then fell to the ground. I finally came to a complete stop.

It was the scariest moment of my life. I sat there and wondered if I had just taken someone's life. Then all of a sudden, the boy stood up and walked to my window. He said, "Ma'am, I am so sorry." I yelled at him and asked him why he ran in front of the bus. He was supposed to get off the bus and stay at the stop until the bus moved He just kept apologizing and then turned and ran into more traffic. It dawned on me that if I had not listened to the Holy Spirit and switched lanes, I would have hit him traveling at almost 60 mph and would not have had time to think or hit my brakes. Because I was obedient and switched lanes, I was allowed a second to see the child running and slow the car down, which is what saved his life.

Later that day, I was still seeing that child's face in my mind. God spoke so clearly to me that evening and said, "When I tell you to switch lanes in life, it's not always for you. Sometimes it is for someone else." I thought, *Wow, God is good! He told me to switch lanes so that child would live.* This is a reminder that we often debate with God without realizing that at that moment, He may be asking us to do something that will benefit ourselves and others, which is sometimes uncomfortable.

The point of changing lanes in this season of my life is so that I can minister to others. God said that I would experience things and partner with key people that I would have never believed would have taken the time for me. All of this will help my ministry. He said I need to stay focused and always take the lanes that will keep me in sync with Him. Sometimes, God has to take us a different route for our own good. All we have to do is be obedient and follow. I can certainly say, the lanes of my life have been interesting and full of surprises.

Chapter 4

New Direction

Dream:

It was getting late in the evening as I walked down the street in a somewhat busy neighborhood. It was a pretty normal neighborhood full of laughter and children playing and people were sitting on their porches and just living life. The only thing confusing about this setting was me was the fact that I was lost. .I was looking for my place. I was trying to get home. At that moment, I didn't really focus on where I had come from at all. I just wanted to find my home. I decided to keep walking and I knew eventually, I would find my place. I had a strong feeling that I was getting close to where I lived. I stopped and looked to my right and knew that this was it. I was home. It wasn't a house or an apartment but a college dorm. I said to myself, *Oh well,* and went inside. I started down the hallway but did not know which room was mine. *Now I'm confused again*, I thought. Looking down this long hallway was a bit intimidating, I must admit. There were four doors in the hallway. I knew that I was supposed to go inside one of them, so I decided to try them all.

I went inside the first door which led me outside in the dark. There was a groundskeeper who met me. He had black holes for eyes and had no voice. I could feel his spirit as he was warning me that this was not the place for me. I thought his being there was very weird. I walked past him to see more of this strange place. He followed me and would not let up on gesturing for me to go back into the hallway. All of a sudden I looked over to my right and saw a family of three. There was a husband, wife, and a small child. The family also had black holes for eyes and they walked around like zombies. It was obvious that they were the walking dead. This family was not alive. I'd finally had enough of the weird situation so I turned, left the room, and went back into the hallway.

When I opened the next door, I surprised a young college girl, who was sitting Indian style on her bed, talking on her cell phone. She looked at me as if I were disturbing her. She yelled, "Get out of my room," and went right back to talking on her phone. She was very mean and seemed to not have a care in the world. So I left and went back into the hallway.

The very next door did not look attractive. It had a dark shadow on it and I could hardly make out the letters on it. I decided to skip that door because it wasn't inviting to me. I opened the next door where I surprised a middle aged woman who had a decent house but was alone, angry, and bitter. She looked at me and said, "You don't belong here." I took my frustration back to the hallway and looked at the only door that I had not been in, which was the unattractive door. I thought to myself, *What if that door is where I am supposed to be?* Then I woke up.

Real Life:

After two years of marriage, one morning my husband woke up and decided that he no longer wanted to be married. I thought my life was over because wasn't something that I was used to seeing. Divorce wasn't common in my family. I didn't know what to do. How was I to pick up the pieces and move on? My original thought before coming to this conclusion was that maybe this was all a joke. I was waiting for the camera crew from the reality joke TV shows to come out. Later that day, I found that my husband was not joking. He really meant that he was done with our marriage. I arrived home from work that evening to a U-Haul parked on my lawn as my husband and his friends were packing things onto the truck. I called my closest friends who came to my rescue. They prayed me through my pain. They ministered to me and gave me a place to stay I began to feel like the state of Mississippi was closing in on me mentally. I felt there was nothing else for me to accomplish there. I needed a change of pace because my husband left me and took the only child that I had, his three year old little girl that I was raising. My sister and her husband had been in Dallas, Texas for a year. They extended an invitation for me to come and stay with them until I could get my life together and get back on my feet. This would take some serious thought and prayer because I had never lived in another state before. I would have to leave my wonderful job in Jackson, give up being around all of my family and friends, and move to a place I have never been, with no job. I told God I had already lost everything. Nothing could be any worse than suffering what I had already suffered. I prayed and asked God, if it was right for me to leave Mississippi, send me a sign.

Interpretation:

The dream confirmed to me that God is on my side and will guide me if I listen. *Teach me to do your will, for you are my God; may your good Spirit lead me on level ground. Psalms 143:10 (NIV).* Throughout the dream, I was trying to find my way home. I wandered and searched and almost went in the wrong direction a couple of times, but each time it happened, He sent me right back to my destiny road. The first door that had the zombie-like family represented myself, my ex-husband, and his child that we were raising. That family was dead and I needed to keep going. The next door had the rude college girl. I realized she was me at that age; I had moved on from that phase of my life, so I had to leave that door.

I skipped the door that looked less attractive because it didn't look like it was for me. The last door with the lonely older woman was me and how I would end up if I did not enter the correct door. I had to go back to the unattractive door in order to get my gift. I opened that door, moved to Texas, and walked right into my blessings! Sometimes our blessings are behind the doors that look less attractive to us. We have to focus on His will for our lives and not focus on the outer beauty.

Psalms 32:8
"I will instruct you and teach you in the way you should go; I will guide you with My eye."

Chapter 5

Houston Journey

Dream:

My house was full of friends and family. I felt surrounded by love. I was so excited about some of my old friends from Mississippi coming to visit me in Texas. They finally arrived that evening, excited about the activities that I had planned. My house was the place where friends and family were always welcome to come, have fun, and relax without question. This evening, a few of them stated that they wanted to go fishing as one of the excursions, and with me being the hostess, it was my duty to provide. I informed them that they could fish in the swimming pool in the back of my house because I was raising fish. I escorted everyone to the back where we shortly realized that fishing may not be possible due to the fact that there was a huge, black catfish, dead in the pool. It was enormous. It was the size of a baby whale. We studied it closely because we thought it was a whale. It turned out to be just that, what we thought, a catfish. We just kind of left it there for the rest of the night and tried to not let it ruin our party.

There were other interesting things happening that evening. As we were enjoying the gathering, there was a beautiful tiger walking amongst us. It was obvious that he was a pet and that he was dear to my heart. It seemed that everyone at the party was comfortable with the tiger. They loved the fact that he was so friendly and so beautiful! However, I was nervous and scared. I kept running from him and hiding in my room the whole night. Everyone was wondering why I was so afraid. How could I run from such a beautiful and peaceful animal? I decided to take a break from running and check on the rest of the party. I found everyone standing around my pool looking in disgust again at the giant dead fish.

Real Life:

    We met online. At first, I didn't pay much attention to him. He had a weird sound on the phone, much like a computer. I am so serious about this. His voice was straight and clear and weird. He was from Nigeria. I loved dating guys from Africa. There was something about their accents that made me excited. The culture that most of them came from was to be respected as well. I can say though, they love women! Our conversations became long and intense. We began to Skype together, which allowed us to see each other on the screen as we talked. He was so handsome with a nice smile and great teeth, which was always my favorite feature. We talked at least four hours a day for about a month before deciding to meet. He lived in Houston and I lived in Dallas. It was a four hour drive to see the man that I was crazy about. He would tell me how he loved educated women who were beautiful. He said the woman he marries will have to love Christ. I was thinking, *Well, I am the perfect one for you.*

We decided to go ahead and meet up. He drove to Dallas. We were both very nervous and excited when we saw each other. We prayed together, talked, ate, and fell in love, all in that order.

After dating for about five months, traveling back and forth, praying, and fasting, we both felt like God was answering our prayers. God wanted us to get married! I kept asking, "Could this be it? Is this it? God, have you finally brought me the man that you want me to have?" Because of my past, I struggled with trust. I often tell people that it is not that I don't trust God, I just don't trust my God-O-Meter! (That's my ability to determine His voice. We were so excited and we asked God to help us with this transition. We wanted more than anything to be close to each other. Either he had to move to Dallas or I had to move to Houston. I began to make preparations to relocate. I started with searching for jobs in Houston. I asked God one more time to send me a sign. "Is this my husband or not?"

After the dream, I thought I had the green light to go ahead and move. My newfound love interest represented the tiger in the dream. I felt like God was trying to tell me, that others around me did not see the gentle and beautiful person that he was.

So... I found a job and an apartment living two miles from the love of my life. It seemed that from day three, he seemed to be distant, not to mention he didn't help me move. I had to hire help because he was too busy. The more I spent time with him and we got closer, I realized he had gotten comfortable with me being around. He would leave his phone lying around. I noticed that he had plenty of women calling him on a regular basis, including a woman who was known by everyone to have AIDS. They used to be roommates, and he would tell me how she made his life a living hell. I read a message on his phone from her one day that led me to believe that they were dating.

That day I also found that he had several side women. He was not faithful to me at all. He would soon become very mean to me as if he didn't want me there. We would argue so much and we'd break up every time we argued. But I kept taking him back, because I felt like I couldn't do any better. *He really loves me. He just has issues.* I kept telling myself. So many women find themselves in this position. The final straw for me was the day he put his hands on me; even then, I didn't leave immediately. I was so broken. He had thrown me across the room and started yelling evil things to me—things to destroy my character and break down my self-esteem. How did I get into this situation? This was a very dark season for me. I had moved away from my family and friends only to be treated like this. This was one of the loneliest times of my life. I kept asking God, "Why me?"

Interpretation:

I realized after moving back to Dallas and getting my life back on track, what God was really saying in the dream. He was trying to warn me of what was to come. The most important thing that I missed was the fact that tigers are beautiful creatures on the outside, but they are also the most vicious and can rip a human being to shreds without reason. Everyone in the dream saw the tiger for what it was, a beautiful, but vicious animal. I was the one who did not see it. The fish in the pool represented the fact that Christ was dead in our relationship.

God loves us enough to give us warnings. He also knows which path we will take. He allowed me to take this path so that I could learn perseverance and patience. It was this experience that reminded me that God can find you anywhere. Even when you feel you are cut off from society and in hiding. You are still visible to him, and He cares enough to help you out of your situation.

James 1:12

"Blessed is the man who endures temptation; for when he has been approved, he will receive the crown of life which the Lord has promised to those who love Him."

Chapter 6

Birthing Destiny

Dream:

I was hanging out with my man in Brandon, Mississippi near the land where my parents lived. We were so in love! We would walk the streets in the country, holding hands and enjoying each other thoroughly.

Our laughter was contagious! I felt like life together couldn't be better. I had a great man, whom I enjoyed. He loved me and I loved him. We decided to attend a gathering in the city with some friends to share in their joy of birthdays for this year. On the way to the event, I noticed my stomach was growing right before my eyes. I yelled out to him that I was pregnant. He said it was impossible because he wasn't the father. I asked him, who else's could it be? And why would he say that? He said, "Because your stomach is growing too fast, that ain't no human." He said something was very weird about this situation.

We arrived at the event and all of a sudden, I wasn't in the mood to have fun anymore. I had just told my man that I was pregnant and he totally denied it was his. I understood that the situation wasn't normal, because my stomach literally grew to seven months in a matter of minutes. But, who else's could it be?

He had no right to act this way. In my mind I was his woman. We left shortly after arriving at the event.

For the next few days, he wasn't there for me. I asked him to rub my feet; he wouldn't. I asked him to cook and clean, he wouldn't. I keep mentioning the fact that bringing a baby into the world takes more than one person, and I needed his help. He was very stubborn and said that I did not need his help. He was not there for me in any way, shape, form, or fashion. It takes a man and woman to bring a child into the world. He said he was not there for the conception and he would not be there for the pregnancy, or the birth.

Real Life:

The guy in this dream is the same guy that I was dating in the previous chapter from Houston. I was going through the thought process of trying to see if he would be the type who would support me in my endeavors in life. I wanted to know if he would be a supportive husband and have my back when I needed him most. So I did as any child who respects her father would do, I asked the Lord if this was a healthy relationship for me.

Interpretation:

The dream clearly shows a man who is uninterested in helping the woman he is with. There are several things wrong with this picture. First, we were not married in the dream; therefore, God was letting me know that he wasn't going to marry me. Also, no woman can grow a baby in her stomach that fast. In the dream, I grew to be seven months pregnant in a matter of minutes. Those types of things can only be done in God's timing and in his supernatural realm. This symbolizes that this wasn't a natural pregnancy, but a supernatural one. God wants to birth something spectacular out of me and it would not be done in human timing but, in His timing and this man was not going to do a thing to help or support it. This man would not have any part in my destiny. He would only get in the way and frustrate me making life even harder.

Well, he turned out to be exactly the way he was in the dream, mean and unsupportive. However, God did say that this birth had nothing to do with this man, and he would not be around. I had peace in knowing that God had my back. But how many times have you been through this? Knowing God has spoken something to you but because you have your own agenda, you decide to help God out and do your own thing? Don't raise your hand, I understand that most of us have done this. I continued to date the man and tried to force him to be my husband. I am here to tell you, when God speaks, listen! If not, there are usually consequences waiting on the other side. It wasn't until after I got out of that situation, that God showed me parts of my destiny and I began to walk in it. I am determined from this point on, to stay on course and trust what God has for me.

Jeremiah 29:11

For I know the plans I have for you," declares the LORD, "plans to prosper you and not to harm you, plans to give you hope and a future. (NIV)

Chapter 7

Unfaithful

Dream:

I was attending a huge church convention with a male friend. We decided to get a hotel room together. It was a big beautiful hotel with beautiful glass chandeliers and it was the hotel where the convention was being held. We were so happy to finally be alone together in a city where no one knew us. All we wanted was to spend time together freely without having to look over our shoulders. I was so happy to be in the presence of the man of my dreams! We checked into our room and I excused myself to go to the restroom.

When I returned, my heart dropped with dread. This was the most embarrassing and shameful situation I had ever been in. I stood in shock as I looked from his face to his wife standing next to him. I immediately began to apologize to her as I grabbed my things to leave the room. She began screaming and yelling. It was as if someone was stabbing her with a dull knife. She looked at me and said, "Yes, you are wrong, but I don't blame you." She then turned and looked at him with great disgust. The pain I saw in her eyes was heart breaking. At that moment, I began to cry for her as I walked out of the hotel room. I stood in the lobby reflecting and asking myself, *How did I get here?* I had never tried to have a relationship with a married man before. I knew better. *How did this come so close to happening?*

At that moment, I didn't want to live anymore. I was disgusted with myself and the fact that I came so close to hurting another human being this badly. I looked up and saw her weeping as her friends were holding her up and half-dragging her because she couldn't walk due to the mental pain I had caused. They walked around that lobby and prayed for her and consoled her and tried to make her snap out of it. For some reason, I was feeling all of the pain she was feeling at that moment. I couldn't stop crying, my head was pounding, my whole body ached, my hands were tingling, I felt worthless, and I wanted to kill myself.

Real Life:

This dream was so real to me that I woke up in pain and had to sit up in bed, calm myself down and convince myself that it was all a dream. It wasn't real, but I could literally feel the pain of this dream. I had a friend and business partner who was married. He was a great guy but he flirted with me. I knew that if I entertained his advances, his marriage would be over. But I stayed strong and ministered to him about how sacred marriage is and how he should respect it. I was able to stay strong and safe by thinking about my God and about his wife. I felt sorry for her and did not want her to suffer as I did. I asked God why did I have that dream and why were the feelings so real?

Interpretation:

God had to remind me of the exact feelings I felt when my ex-husband cheated on me and left me. When I went through that same storm back in 2005/2006 I remembered the pain being so great, I wouldn't have wished it on my worst enemy. The reality is, I am a single, attractive woman and I am approached by married men all of the time. God doesn't want us to fall into temptation. He always sends us warning signs. Thank you, Lord! It is so great that God cares enough about me to send me warnings and keep me from hitting some of the brick walls in life.

1 Corinthians 10:13

"No temptation has overtaken you except such as is common to man; but God is faithful, who will not allow you to be tempted beyond what you are able, but with the temptation will also make the way of escape, that you may be able to bear it."

Chapter 8

Back for Validation

Dream:

My sister and I, along with a cousin decided to go play laser tag. We arrived at the building only to find that there was a long line inside. We bought our tickets and stood in line. While in line, there were small stations that we had to visit for various reasons. Some stations asked to see the tickets that we purchased in the beginning. Half way through, I stopped by one of the trash cans to throw away some trash from the food that we had eaten while waiting in line.

When I could not locate my ticket, I realized that I had thrown it away with the trash. I remember thinking, *I must get back to the trash can to sift through the trash to find my ticket, so that I will have access to play laser tag.* I really wanted to find the ticket, to gain entry into the laser tag area. I began to think, surely the rest of the stations would allow me to go through, knowing that at some point I had to have had my ticket to have gotten this far. So I thought, there is no point in going back to search for it in the trash. I would just take my chances.

Before getting to the next station, I wandered out of one of the side exit doors and ended up outside the building. It was the weirdest thing, I saw my bicycle from home lying on the ground. I couldn't figure out how it got there or why. So I picked it up and searched for a safe place to park it. The environment seemed to be familiar; I knew I was just outside the campus of Jackson State University, which is my alma mater. My focus now was to figure out how these things appeared and why. But, my main focus is get back inside the laser tag building, because I knew eventually my sister and cousin would be looking for me. As I started back towards the building, I was walking through an old apartment complex. I recognized a family that I grew up with from my neighborhood in Mississippi. I was so happy to see this family that I had not seen in years. As a matter of fact, one of the young ladies who was about two years older than me was adamant about making sure that I knew that she had died twice and came back.

She was so excited about the fact that this had happened to her. She really wanted to convince me. The more I thought about it, I tried to convince her that I remembered her dying in a car accident, and not coming back, because her mother was currently raising her kids. As I looked closely look at the situation, her face did not look the same, she almost looked like a totally different person. I did not think that she was the same family member we all knew. But I was wondering why all of the family around her thought it was really her. I felt she was trying to trick us all. I did not think that she was the same young lady that we all knew. But I was wondering, why was I the only one who could see that she was lying. Was this an imposter? They eventually took me back to the laser tag building from which I had wandered away from. I really wanted to get back inside because I figured my sister and cousin would be looking for me soon. I wanted to go back to the trash can inside to search for my ticket so that I could get back in line to get in to play laser tag. But as soon as I got out of their car, and thanked the family for the ride, I walked around the building and there were my sister and cousin greeting me.

Real Life:

At this time in my life, I was dealing with the pain of rejection. I knew that I was a talented individual. God gave me the gift of worshiping Him through my singing. I didn't have a problem so much with those who had heard me minister, it was those who had never heard me minister. Because of the nature of my job as an assistant, people viewed me as just that, an assistant in the music world. I constantly had to fight with various musicians and other people trying to prove that I was talented and important. I tried to show others that I was educated and more than just an assistant, but people still over looked me. I have been through so much in my life, both good and bad which contributed to me being such a wise person. I found myself always trying to convince others that the things that I have seen and the lessons that I have learned would help them with what they were going through.

Interpretation:

The line that we were waiting in symbolizes that whatever I am waiting on is coming and the line is getting shorter. The reason I got off course is because I lost focus. I still made my way back, but I had to start over like Jonah in the belly of the whale. This is a message that tells me I must stay focused. The bicycle represents my current new love for life, as I have started cycling and loving it. My old college being there represents my past life, as well as the family I knew from my past. My wanting to go back to the garbage can to get validation is true in real life. I want validation so that others will see that I belong I am constantly having to try and prove to people in the industry that I am in, that I am smart, talented, and competent. Most think I home just a Mississippi country girl who was raised on a farm and don't know anything. To get respect, I have to state my education and experience. This represents what I have been fighting with in the past few months. God says I don't have to reach back into my past to be validated. I sure don't have to reach into the trash for my validation either. The ones who are supposed to see me, will see me. It is normal to not be accepted by others. In fact, it usually means you are carrying something valuable. The anointing is a powerful thing! It draws people to you while keeping away others who want to bring you harm. Your gift will make room for you and those who need to see it, will. Thank you, God for the reminder!

Isaiah 41:10

"So do not fear, for I am with you; do not be dismayed, for I am your God. I will strengthen you and help you; I will uphold you with my righteous right hand." (NIV)

Chapter 9

Unprepared for the Game

Dream:

It was that time of year again. Time for the green and gold Tigers of McLaurin High School to hit the basketball court! We were getting ready for our first game of the season, which was really late for basketball season, since it was close to January. We were being coached by my favorite old coach, Melanie Black. I paid attention to the team as we continued to get dressed at my parents' house in my parents' room. I remember the old team with Fran and Monica. It seemed that I didn't have all of my uniform and I felt like I was too out of shape to play.

I was going to play anyway because as point guard, the team needed me. We were also getting ready to play our biggest rival, Florence High School. I had no choice but to try and play without all of my uniform. To play I needed a white t-shirt to wear under my uniform. I asked everyone I could find if I could borrow a white t-shirt for the game. I searched my house, looking in drawers and I could not find what I needed in order to play the game. I knew that without the rest of my uniform, I would have to sit out. I was unprepared for this game.

Real Life:

This dream hit me at a time in my life when my faith was very low. My communication with God was low. I was deeply saddened because I couldn't find a full-time job. I needed money. Bills were piling up. I was well qualified for the jobs that I was applying for and I was wondering, *Where is God? Why isn't He answering? Why aren't people calling me back about these jobs? What am I doing wrong?*

Interpretation:

Trust God for your preparation. Sometimes we need extra time to prepare. We need to get ready to receive our blessing. We may need to expand our mind capacity to receive. Put on the full armor of God so that you will be ready in season and out of season. If you are going to play the game of life and win, you must be prepared. To have what you need, stay prayed up, spend time with Christ and follow His lead.

Proverbs 24:27
"Prepare your work outside; get everything ready for yourself in the field, and after that build your house" (ESV)

Chapter 10

Transportation Thief

Dream:

My boss was at the barber shop getting his usual haircut. It was normal for him to forget something at home and then ask me to bring it to him. I drove to the barber shop to drop off what he had forgotten. There was a parking lot adjacent to the building, but I parked on the street instead since I would only be running in for a minute. I hoped no one would mess with my little black Civic! I had to pray since we were in the middle of the hood. I went inside the building and located my boss, sitting in the barber's chair. After saying hello to a few of the barbers, I glanced outside to check on my car and noticed it was not there. *Maybe I am looking out of the wrong window,* I thought.

I looked out of another window and my car still wasn't there. *Ok, maybe I am on the wrong side of the building.* I panicked and ran to the door, only to discover that my car in fact had been stolen. I asked everyone inside and outside of the building if they had seen who took my car. I even asked the guys who were on the corner singing just before I went inside, and they said no. I thought about it, and decided they had to have seen something, because they were standing right behind where I parked. I specifically remembered speaking to them when I arrived. When I returned they were in the same spot. But they denied everything. People like to live by the saying, "No one likes a snitch", but who was going to know if any information was given to me?

My biggest concern about my car being stolen was my laptop and iPad were inside. I wasn't so much worried about the car because I knew my insurance would replace it. I did not want to alarm my boss or make him nervous while he was still in the barber's chair, so I waited until he was ready to leave. When he walked outside he seemed baffled to see me still standing there on the sidewalk. He asked, "What are you still doing here?" I responded that my car had been stolen. He rushed towards the side of the building where he left his car. He looked all around for it. Now boss' car was missing. He discovered that his vehicle had been stolen as well from the parking lot

His face began to turn red as he got upset. But that was short-lived because, his thought process was, he wouldn't miss the vehicle. Out of all the vehicles at his house, his Hummer was not one of his favorites. We both walked back to the building to make a report to the owners of the barber shop while waiting for the police to come.

Interpretation:

    I am a worship leader. God placed me under one of the greatest worship leaders in the industry to learn and develop my ministry. It has been a wonderful experience. The road has been both rough and smooth. I truly understand now how the enemy focuses on attacking worship leaders. We are doing the very work that Lucifer used to do. The Bible says that he used to be the greatest. I often pray for my boss and his peace of mind, because the enemy sure has it out for him as he does all of us. My boss is a faithful servant of God, and I am his servant. I truly believe that if you serve in excellence and serve all of your heart, you will be rewarded. Just like Elisha, Elijah's servant, I also prayed for a double portion of his anointing in the music and ministry. My prayer is that when people hear my music, they will feel the anointing and began to worship Christ our Lord.

    I believe this dream was a wonderful reminder from God. He wants to remind me of where I am headed in life. The same thing that happened to my boss, happened to me in the dream. Because of the territory that I am currently in under my boss, I will experience some of the same things that he has experienced on his musical journey, but I hope to be prepared for them after walking through some of the fires. His being at the barber shop in the chair, symbolizes him getting his glory, he gets taken care of. Because I'm in the same territory, the same things that he is subject to, I am also subject to as well. By stealing my transportation, the enemy tried to stop me from getting to my destination. The reason no one wanted to tell me what happened including those who had to have seen something, is because they too see how God is blessing me. They want to block me from seeing the promise land. I am so glad that God can get through any block!

2 Kings 2:9

When they had crossed, Elijah said to Elisha, "Tell me, what can I do for you before I am taken from you?" "Let me inherit a double portion of your spirit," Elisha replied (NIV).

Chapter 11

My Wedding

Dream:

Everyone was gathered at my parents' house in Mississippi. I was so excited my cousins, aunts, uncles, and old friends came to celebrate my wedding day with me. My aunts and cousins were helping to get things together to prepare for the reception part of the wedding. I had to sneak and help with the work because they would not let me work on my wedding day. Once everything was done, we all sat around the table and waited. We were waiting for everyone to come from the church where the wedding had just taken place. As I looked around the giant table looking at my family, I was proud to see them supporting me on such a special day. My dad was sitting there with his usual half grin of approval on his face. While we were waiting for the rest of the wedding party, the groom, and the guests, I saw a disturbance from the corner of my eye out of the window. There was a maroon, old school mustang outside. It seemed to be on fire. I saw a little smoke and huge flames coming from under the car, but the car itself was not burning up. One of my brothers saw the fire and tried to put it out with the water hose but it did not work. The sight was a little strange but no one else in the house paid attention to it.

Finally, people began to show up at the house and we were eager to get my reception started. I was totally confused at this point because the groom didn't come and all of sudden, I had no memory of my wedding that supposedly had taken place about an hour ago at the church. I began to look at my family sitting at the table and some of them began to look different. It seemed that they transformed into a white family from Austin, Texas right before my eyes. They were the family of an old co-worker of mine named Heather. Then all of a sudden, Heather walked in wearing a beautiful, white, wedding dress, her face glowing with the happiness of being newly married. I woke up, confused. Was this not my wedding?

Real Life:

I woke up praying, Lord, you are going to have to help me with this one! See at that time in my life, I was dating someone who I thought was a good guy. I asked God to send me a sign so that I would know that it was Him speaking. *Let me know whether I am supposed to marry this man or not.*

Interpretation:

In the beginning, I thought this was my wedding and everyone acted accordingly. The dream later revealed that it was not mine. However, the line is getting shorter and my time is coming, just not now. There were several clues that I should have caught on to like, why was I working at my own reception? Where was my husband? In the dream, I never saw his face and he never came to the reception. If we just had a wedding, wouldn't we be at the reception together? If this was my wedding, why wasn't I dressed? Because this was not my wedding! The sign from God was the car that was on fire, but wasn't burning up, just like the burning bush in the Bible. I got the message from the dream, but was glad that God stamped it with his signature with a miracle that only He could perform, so I would know that this dream was His voice answering my prayer.

Deuteronomy 4:36
"From heaven he made you hear his voice to discipline you. On earth he showed you his great fire, and you heard his words from out of the fire" (NIV)

Chapter 12

Tool Store Vacation

Dream:

My sister, Amy and our first cousin, Kimberly and I were on a vacation out of town. It seemed like we may have been in Florida or maybe some tropical place because I saw palm trees. There were beaches and beautiful scenery. We stopped by a small tool store, just to pick up some supplies. We hung out there for a little while. We were in no hurry because we were on vacation. Kimberly went outside to do something. Amy and I noticed a white vehicle pulling up very slowly with a couple of guys in it. They looked real suspicious. It was just like in the movies when someone is about to do a drive-by shooting.

They looked very weird, and one of them was a Hispanic male with black holes for eyes and a hoodie. All of their eyes were black holes. The Hispanic man began shooting at the building just as Kimberly was heading back inside. She was hit by one of the bullets but didn't get hurt; it did not affect her. She ran back inside and we were all nervous that they would come back and finish the job.

As we watched out of the window, the vehicle came back. We panicked, then I remembered that I had left my pistol at home.

We all reminded Amy that she had hers and needed to use it. She pulled it out and began to fire back. When they realized that we had the power to fight back, they drove off and left us alone. At that moment, we were all shaken up. We just sat there and looked at each other in disbelief, wondering who those men were, why they choose us, and how could this have happened to us? We were so distraught we decided the vacation was over. We packed up the next day and left.

Interpretation:

The hardest thing to remember when we are in trouble is the fact that God has already given us the power to fight back. We just don't access it. In this dream, the black holes for eyes represent the fact that they were sent by the enemy. They were sent to kill and destroy us. This is a case of the enemy trying to take us out. But God has not given us the spirit of fear, but He has given us the power to fight back. Sometimes we have to stop focusing on the problem and focus on our help, which is given by our Lord!

Psalm 144:1
"Of David. Praise be to the LORD my Rock, who trains my hands for war, my fingers for battle." (NIV)

Chapter 13

Enemy at the Court

Dream:

My boss and I were at a basketball game. It was more of an outdoor event, the court that you would find in most urban cities where the community could come and play basketball. I was helping him put on his socks and shoes, and getting him ready to play. I was going to play as well. We were also hyping up our team and getting them ready for what was to come. The time was about 5:00 p.m. We were all excited about playing, although we were a bit tired from previous games.

Just outside of the gates, I noticed a large black head peeking up out of the grass. The head kept watching us and trying to see what we were doing. Then all of a sudden it started coming towards the court and its body began to follow, it was a large, gigantic snake. It was about two feet wide. The closer it got to the court its body kept getting longer and longer. Once it reached the basketball court it began to circle around the court and again, its body never got shorter and the snake kept its eyes on us the whole time while surrounding the court.

I was watching it closely, and looking for the moment that I could yell for everyone to take off running. The strangest thing was that my boss and no one else noticed the giant snake surrounding the court. I questioned everyone and asked why they did not see the snake. It looked like it wanted to devour us. I thought, *How could you guys not see something so big, black, and evil?* Everyone thought I was crazy, and seeing things.

Real Life:

I was awakened out of this dream by the text message notification on my phone. It was my boss stating that he needed to meet with the team immediately. This was rare because it was 12 noon and he had never called a meeting with us before while being out on the road. So my gut feeling told me that something was really wrong. I felt like my dream had something to do with this meeting we were about to have. Sure enough, it was about something that I was being blamed for by the newest employee and staff Of course it was something I didn't do.

He had only been there two months. I had a bad vibe about him from the beginning but no one else felt it. The meeting was about me not being trustworthy. I was so upset by the meeting, I felt my blood pressure rising. The new employee worked with us for a few more months and during that time, everyone began to see his true colors. He was the evil snake surrounding our court.

He wanted to devour us. He tried his plan of tearing the company down. For some reason, he hated me and the boss. He spoke evil things about us. But it did not work!

God sent that message as a warning which actually caused me to pay close attention to the evil in our camp. I am honored that God chose me as the messenger to the camp.

Luke 6:22

"Blessed are you when people hate you, when they exclude you and insult you and reject your name as evil, because of the Son of Man." (NIV)

Chapter 14

My Best Friend

Dream:

It was getting late in the evening, about 7:00 p. m., right around dinner time. I was driving home thinking I should do a pop-up at my best friend's house. We really hadn't spoken in a while, but her husband had emailed me an invite several weeks before. I decided that I would stop by anyway on this particular day. I knocked on the door; her husband answered the door and he and the children were very happy to see me. We all have history together. We had been through a couple of fires in life together. I walked into the living room and said hello to my friend. She smiled and gave me a quick hug. It was obvious there was still a little distance between us, but we were happy to see each other. The family was preparing to eat dinner. They asked if I would stay and eat with them. I said yes. We laughed and shared stories and apologized to each other for any wrong doings or misunderstandings. We truly missed each other.

Real Life:

I had a best friend that I had grown up with. We were also family, raised in the same neighborhood and church. We had always been there for each other. We went to college together and were even roommates for a while. Her children were my children, I helped her take care of them because the father wasn't helpful at all. Of course I understand that friends outgrow each other, but in this situation, we were family and family can't leave! You just deal with each other in other ways. I really could not put my finger on what happened between us. For some reason, she stopped calling, texting, and answering my calls. She never gave me an explanation for the change. I could only assume what the problem was. I kept asking her siblings if she had mentioned my name or even told them what she had against me, but no one knew the answer. I was devastated to know that I possibly could have done something to hurt someone in my family. There were a couple of mutual friends in our lives at that time who may have had a hand in the possible, intentional destruction of our friendship. But I did not know for sure, so I decided to back away, give her some time and leave it in God's hands. I prayed about it at least every month when I thought about her and family

Interpretation:

    My answer from God was I needed to go through the head of the family. Her husband wanted us to make up all along. Maybe he thought that our issue was senseless. After having this dream, I had hoped that God would restore the communication between us. I knew that it would happen through her husband making the connection. The saying goes, "Time heals all wounds."

Well, after a few years, I sent an email to her husband, apologizing and asking him to speak with her about talking to me. I told him that I wanted to know what I had done. The next week, she called me and apologized for making me feel that way all of these years. I accepted her apology but never asked exactly what happened. I was ok with letting it go and letting the past be the past. I am glad I listened to the Father and did it His way.

Proverbs 19:21
"There are many plans in a man's heart, nevertheless the Lord's council that will stand." (NKJV)

Chapter 15

My Husband or Not

Dream:

We had just gotten married about a week ago; I don't remember the actual wedding. I just remember seeing his ring. His hand was very large. It was bigger than his whole body. His body seemed really frail and weak. We were happy, comfortable and in love. We were about to travel to our new home where we would begin our new lives together back in the state of Mississippi. We had visited a few of our close friends in Dallas who were married, just to hang out and say goodbye. We thanked them for everything they had done for us. It was obvious that I was married to this man, but it seemed my eyes kept focusing on his hand and his gold wedding band. He kept wanting me to look at his ring. Not just look, but really focus on it. Every situation and every setting in the dream, his hand kept waving around in my view, displaying his wedding band. It seemed to be a reminder that we were married. The whole focus of the dream was the two of us and our marriage.

Real Life:

This dream came at a time when I was dating a minister

from Mississippi and I was really seeking God to see if this was the man that I was supposed to spend the rest of my life with. We had known each other for about nine years and had become casual friends in 2005. He had always been in my life, but we didn't start dating until October 2012. He was the ex-fiancé of one of my really good friends, so this was really a strange relationship to me. I knew some people would be uneasy about it, so I really needed God to step in and speak clearly. He had spoken to me many times, but I felt like this time He was saying, "Come on, Autumn get it! What else do I have to do to get you to see what I am telling you?" When I awakened from this dream at about 3:00 a.m., I asked God to confirm again through his word. I immediately opened my Bible and it was sitting on *Ephesians 5:24,* "Now as the church submits to Christ, so also wives should submit to their husbands in everything." *(NIV)*

Interpretation:

God said to me, "If you marry this man—and you can, because I give you the freedom to choose—you must be ready to submit to him in everything." That means, whatever his problems are, will eventually be my problems. Whatever he suffers with, I will suffer with. I had to think that whatever is wrong now, will be magnified in marriage. His waving the ring was a warning to say, "Autumn, you must really think about this. Once you are in, you are in."

I remember in the dream, the feeling of not wanting to leave the state. He wanted to take me back to my past. I had a very painful past while living in the state of Mississippi. This dream showed me that he was mentally and spiritually going to take me back to my past. As a matter of fact, he ended up doing to me what my past had done. I am so glad I did not marry him and go back. Thank you, Lord, for the warning!

There is great excitement when we have something great to share or someone we are enjoying. We want to show the world. I want to invite you to know my Savior! Because of Him, my journey in life has been amazing. He walks with me, talks with me, and guides me through every step. I can be hard headed most times. I am not always obedient which may result in me experiencing great pain and consequences, but with each trial, God sees me through and He gets the glory out of each lesson learned. I can't help but get excited about my personal relationship with such a personal God, and I want all to experience the same closeness! He will speak to you if you spend time with Him as you praise and acknowledge Him. Your confession and belief in

Jesus Christ gives you physical access into heaven for eternity, and your relationship with Him now gives you mental access while on Earth.

Revelation 3:20

"Behold, I stand at the door and knock. If anyone hears My voice and opens the door, I will come in to him and dine with him, and he with Me." (NKJV)

Romans 10:9

"That if you confess with your mouth the Lord Jesus and believe in your heart that God has raised Him from the dead, you will be saved." (NKJV)

Chapter 16

The Pool Experience

Dream:

The time was about five o'clock in the evening; Selena and I were at an apartment complex in Dallas. We were so excited about taking our children swimming. We were in the locker room getting them dressed for the pool. I was laughing and playing with my boys who were being silly. They were so excited about going swimming with Selena's children. We were going to allow the kids to play all day. After getting the children dressed, I took them out to the pool to meet with the other kids. I found a comfortable spot to sit, put on my sunglasses and then woke up.

Real Life:

Days went by and I really did not seek to find the answer to why I had that particular dream. It didn't mean that much to me. However, at that time in my life, I was preparing to make the move to Houston to be near who I thought was my future husband. I felt I had heard from God and everything was set. The only thing left was to talk to the people at my apartment complex in Dallas about my leaving. One day I walked into the front office of my apartment complex; the manager saw me in the lobby and invited me into her office. I walked in and immediately went to the window, noticing that the swimming pool was closed. I asked her why this was so. She said that the pool was under construction. I thought that was very interesting, because just yesterday the pool was working beautifully. Then I looked at her and realized her name tag read, Selena. She asked for my name and with my response, she gave me a weird look. After a long pause she said, "Autumn, I had a dream about you. Do you wear colored contacts?" I said, "Yes, I normally do, but at the moment I have an eye infection and I'm forced to wear my glasses for a while." She said, "In my dream we were preparing to go swimming, but you had on contacts rather than the glasses I see on you now." I just stared at her in amazement, knowing that I'd had the same dream a few days ago. She said what really made things weird is the fact that I came right into her office and inquired about the swimming pool. I honestly did not know what to think about this encounter. I prayed for her and then left.

Interpretation:

The word I heard was, "The excitement Selena had in knowing that you wear contacts represents the fact that you are in similar places in your lives (a similar season). The two of you in the locker room getting the children dressed is literally God making us ready to go deeper—thus the pool. The pool is under construction specifically for you in this next season of your life. The pool is the journey being tailor made just for you and you will go deeper with God than you've ever been." The contacts in your eyes in her dream also represent the fact that God wants to give you both clearer vision and new sight and for that to happen, the color contacts are gonna go away so that what is true can be revealed. In other words, to really see clearly you have to train your eyes in a specific way. Selena is gonna need to see parts of your journey so that she can learn to navigate the waters of her own pool time with God. The pool also represents boundaries. You won't be allowed to go too far. This pool time is training and teaching you how to swim and dive, so that when you head to the ocean, you will not drown; because you will already be comfortable with deep waters.

"This next year is the start of a new season and new process in your life. This season will last 5-7 years and during that time, you will go places with God that you have never imagined. Trust Him and obey. It will seem odd at times, but it is really important that you submit and respond to His guidance and instruction. He wants all of you. Give it. Nothing less is gonna be acceptable."

1 Peter 5:6-7

"Humble yourselves, therefore, under God's mighty hand, that he may lift you up in due time. Cast all your anxiety on him because he cares for you" (ESV.)

Chapter 17

Showtime

It is a wonderful thing to have people speak to God on your behalf or for God to send messages to you through other people. This is not a reason for us not to go to God on our own, but sometimes He uses this process to confirm things to us, especially if we are in situations where we can't hear clearly from Him.

A young lady from my church named Verda once told me that she had a dream about me. Of course I was really interested in what she had to say. She said she was at a huge arena accompanied by some of our friends and church family. The reason for being at the arena was to attend some type of celebration or concert. She said they could see me waiting back stage for my turn to hit the stage in front of all the world. She said I was wearing a beautiful white dress, my hair and makeup were perfect. She said she doesn't know exactly what I was getting ready to do, but it was obvious that the audience was there to see me. They were all excited and waiting for me to come out.

Interpretation:

I shared Verda's dream with my dream interpreter, and she

said, "Autumn, I know exactly what this dream means." She said, "The event represents your life. The people around are watching how your life unfolds. This next season for you will be one that is lived openly in the public eye. Your life will be lived in front of others so that they know God's power through your life. Perfect hair and makeup means you're prepared to go out and perform. Do the work of this next season."

Real Life:

I was at a standstill in my life when this dream was told to me. My career wasn't taking me anywhere that I could see. I was tired of punching the same clock every day at a job that was making me unhappy. I had a lot of dreams and aspirations to be something great! I was not great at my current job, because I was not operating in my calling. I needed to do the very thing that God called me to do. I knew the calling on my life, but I questioned myself, *How am I supposed to get there?*

It was confirmed to me then, my life was destined to be great. I really needed to make sure I was living right because of the focus from the public that would soon be on my life. I certainly do not want to steer people into darkness. This message was strongly connected to my writing and music careers. Thank you, Lord for your confirmation to keep going and not give up.

I know sometimes it is hard to believe when other people say God told them something to tell you. These two young ladies never said, "God said." They just told me the story and I knew it was from Him because He had already revealed it to me.

Numbers 12:6
"And he said, 'Hear my words: If there is a prophet among you, I the Lord make myself known to him in a vision; I speak with him in a dream'" (ESV).

Conclusion

Life is a highway on which we need very strong guidance. There is so much we can fall into that we may not be able to bounce back from. I certainly don't understand how people are able to get along without Christ in their lives. He is the GPS for our souls to follow through storms and heavy rain. God gave me a vision to share with others about how both simple and complicated life can be. Picture this: We are all traveling on one big highway with curves, exits and speed bumps. We exit life's highway for various reasons. Sometimes, we get weary and exit to take a break.

We are guilty of reading the signs wrong, thinking they say something else. How many of us are guilty of getting off to find a shortcut that doesn't work and then we have to find our way back to where we were. Then some exit for a pit stop and to do a little shopping. The wonderful thing is, almost every exit has a fueling station for rejuvenating purposes.

There are times we see people on the side of the road having car trouble, but we never stop to help because we fear for our own lives, so we pass by and leave them suffering. There are speed bumps that are made to slow us down to make us think. Curves are twists and turns that give us a little excitement along the way. There is heavy traffic sometimes.

There are so many situations and opportunities on the highway that we can experience, good and bad. The fact of the matter is that the highway is always there. We all must travel it. The dangers seen and unseen will always be there, so it's wise to travel with our spiritual GPS. Sometimes it is hard to understand the GPS, but if we hang in there long enough and let it take us around the closed roads and traffic jams, the GPS will always recalculate and get us back on track! Our Lord and Savior, Jesus Christ is our GPS! Through him, we have access to the Father. Do you trust Him?

Sweet Dreams

Now I lay me down to sleep, waiting to hear your voice, had a long day of sin and shame, I'm so sorry for my bad choice.

You tapped me on my shoulder today and tried to whisper a word, Ignored your voice and even your touch, my last backslide was September third.

Tests and trials are for me to see, how great oh Lord you are! You always step in and fight my battles, for every single war!

I have gotten better with praise and worship to offer You, my King. I admit sometimes we are ever so lazy, with our worship songs to sing.

You're a faithful God and constant friend whose ways won't change. How do you deal with unstable me, when I'm always giving you pain?

I know my life could be easier, if I changed a few little simple things. You've taken the time and patience with me to give me somewhere to lean.

Of course not onto my own understanding, my trust is on stable ground. My trust in You is all I have, no greater love have I ever found.

It's weighing heavy on my mind, to ask You why it is You chose me. Don't get me wrong I'm super glad, because I could have not been free.

You speak to me in several ways, to get messages to your people. Sometimes I really don't want to share, even under the great big steeple.

I am certainly an empty vessel and I am glad You are using me, For every valley I have fallen in, it was for Your glory, now I see.

After reading your word just right now, I'll close my eyes to sleep. I'll meet you at our special place, my head, my heart, my dreams.

www.ingramcontent.com/pod-product-compliance
Lightning Source LLC
LaVergne TN
LVHW051154080426
835508LV00021B/2632